I TOUCHED A CAT AND I LIKED IT

I TOUCHED A CAT AND I LIKED IT

BY ANNA BLANDFORD

Hardie Grant

BOOKS

DEDICATED TO GARETH,
BECAUSE HE STILL DEALS WITH
THE KITTY LITTER TRAYS

CONTENTS

WELCOME TO MY BOOK, FEATURING ALL MY FAVOURITE CAT THINGS.

I fly my cat-loving flag proudly. I will cross the road to pat a cat. My friend in France often sends me photos of cats she spots in her neighbourhood. I'm only ever tagged in cat-related things on Facebook. My Instagram feed is largely made up of cat accounts, and I also have my own Instagram account dedicated to our cat, Bubsy. I am happy to report that since having kids I still take a lot of photos of the cat.

My two children are obsessed with cats too. They both began calling them 'mees' when they first learned to talk. Recently my youngest, Dougie, spotted one while we were walking at night. He shouted 'MEES!' and pointed wildly, and sure enough, there was a cat, in the dark, looking at us. Proud parenting moment!

I have a collection of cat figurines I've been gathering since I was young, which I display proudly in my 'cat shrine'. The kids demand to be lifted to see the 'mees' and carefully give the less fragile ones a wee kiss.

MY CAT-LOVING JOURNEY BEGAN IN THE 1980s.

Growing up, we had two pet cats that my parents had adopted
before I was born, but they were getting old and Mum decided
we needed more cats. I still remember how happy I was when she
told me we would be getting two new kittens. We found Bootsy,
a sweet but cross-looking cat, through an ad in the paper, and
Smudge came from a family who lived on a nearby farm.

Exciting news,
kids: we're
getting two
new kittens!

Best news ever!

Smudge was almost feral and we had a hard time trying to
catch her to take her home. She was so scared and gave us a
few frightful experiences of our own, such as the time when she
ran into our fireplace, or when she hid in the septic tank. I was
pretty heartbroken as I had imagined a friendly pet, not one that
required me to spend my Saturday afternoon sitting alongside a
septic tank, pestering her to come out.

However, a few weeks in something changed and Smudge turned
into one of the friendliest and most loving cats. She would put
her arms around my shoulders and hug me, climb trees with me
and join me for adventures on our family farm.

Smudge would jump onto my windowsill at night for pats. Bootsy, her loyal sidekick, would follow along.

IN 1995 MY YOUNGER SISTER, ELIZA, DISCOVERED THAT 'KITTY' SOUNDS QUITE LIKE 'ECHIDNA' OVER THE PHONE.

Eliza found a tiny orange kitten at her primary school and decided she wanted to keep him. The teacher asked her to phone home for permission. My Nanna answered and heard 'echidna' instead of 'kitty' and told Eliza yes, she could bring the echidna home.

When Eliza got to the car that afternoon, Nanna was confused — this wasn't the echidna she had agreed to over the phone. She was suddenly very concerned she had made a family decision way above her pay grade and worried what our mum would think when she arrived home from work.

Mum, can we keep the kitten?

Absolutely not, we already have two cats.

Wait, this is the kitten? This delightful orange creature who just winked at me? We are keeping the kitten!

Pumpkin could fit on the palm of your hand and would wink at you.

Nanna ended up having a love-hate relationship with Pumpkin. Each Tuesday Nanna would come over to visit and Pumpkin would irritate her, getting under her feet and meowing at the door. Despite this, she still brought him meaty treats and loved spoiling him with them.

IN 2013 I ACHIEVED ONE OF MY ULTIMATE LIFE GOALS: I TAMED A FERAL CAT.

We knew we had achieved fully tamed status when I could pick Bubsy up.

Ever since I was a kid I dreamt of taming a feral cat. One day I found a cat at the office and saw my opportunity. We called her Bubsy as a silly name, but it ended up sticking.

I was worried about my partner's allergies and bringing a stray cat to live in an apartment, but in the end Bubsy won out.

TIP:
A cardboard box is not a suitable enclosure to transport a feral cat to the vet.

A month or so after we brought Bubsy home, my dad commented that she would probably always be a bit feral and would never sit on anyone's lap. A few years later, she jumped up on his lap. It was a proud day.

Bubsy thrived on inner-city apartment living, basking in the morning sun. Her feralness slowly disappeared, as did our need to use Urine Off.

Gone are the days of the scrappy little feral cat who would run away from you. Bubsy is now a portly, middle-aged cat who loves nothing more than sleeping in an unmade bed all day, or curling up on your lap at night and keeping you warm.

IN 2015 I ACHIEVED ANOTHER ULTIMATE LIFE GOAL: I CONVERTED SOMEONE (MY PARTNER, GARETH) INTO A FULLY FLEDGED CAT LOVER.

2002–2013: THE NO-CAT YEARS

I'm not really into cats — they're kinda aloof.

I'm also kinda allergic.

2013: WE ADOPT OUR FIRST CAT

Can we have a rule? Bubsy can't come onto the bed.

ONE WEEK LATER

She's on the bed. This is awesome!

2015: FULL CONVERSION HAS OCCURED

I've tamed another stray at the office. I know we have a three-month-old baby, but I want to adopt her.

My face is all itchy — I just rubbed it in Cricket's belly a bunch.

You know they're fully converted when they spend hours sitting in the tub in a chilly bathroom holding a recently neutered cat, their own comfort secondary to that of the cat.

IN 2010 I DREW MY FIRST CAT CARD.

In 2009 Gareth and I started a greeting card business called Able And Game. One year in, Gareth had an idea for a card: a fat cat sitting on a couch with beer, crisps and the TV remote with the message 'I love you just the way I am'. I wasn't sure how it would be received, but we took it to a market and it sold out. We started selling more and more cat cards, and then began making a yearly cat calendar.

In 2013 I was designing cards for an upcoming trade show while I was jet-lagged. I felt like I was officially out of ideas and would never make a decent card again. While I was mucking around, I doodled a wholesome picture of a man patting a cat paired with the text 'I touched a cat and I liked it'. I sat laughing at the drawing for a good while but definitely didn't think I would make it into a card. After laughing some more, I decided I would print a small run to take to our weekly market that weekend. Straight away a woman purchased it for her husband, because that morning he had managed to pat their neighbour's usually unfriendly cat. Then someone else bought it, then someone else, and I realised the card was a winner.

In 2014 my mum travelled up to Brisbane with me to help run a market stall. Setting up the products she commented that we had too many cat things. After two days of chatting to all the cat lovers in Brisbane, she told me she now understood why we made cat products and that actually we needed to make more, not less. Chatting cats with our customers is one of my favourite things about running Able And Game. Sometimes people send me photos of their cats next to our products and it really does make my day.

Hopefully you agree I am well certified to write this book on the subject of cats. Please enjoy, ideally with a cat on your lap.

Sometimes when a cat is sitting down and their tail moves it looks like a strange furry snake.
Cats have night-vision laser eyes.
Behind a cat's ear is the area that contains the softest, silkiest fur.
The Safe Patting Zone: you can usually pat most cats on their backs and they'll be very happy with this.
Whiskers help cats determine how wide they are so they can avoid the embarrassment of the clumsy reverse.
The Danger Patting Zone: many cats do not like to be patted on their back legs.
FUN FACT: The belly sag or 'primordial pouch' is used to protect internal organs during a fight.
Cats' paws are super cute, but they also contain the Danger Spikes.

THE ULTIMATE GUIDE TO CATS

HOW DANGEROUS IS PATTING YOUR CAT'S BELLY?

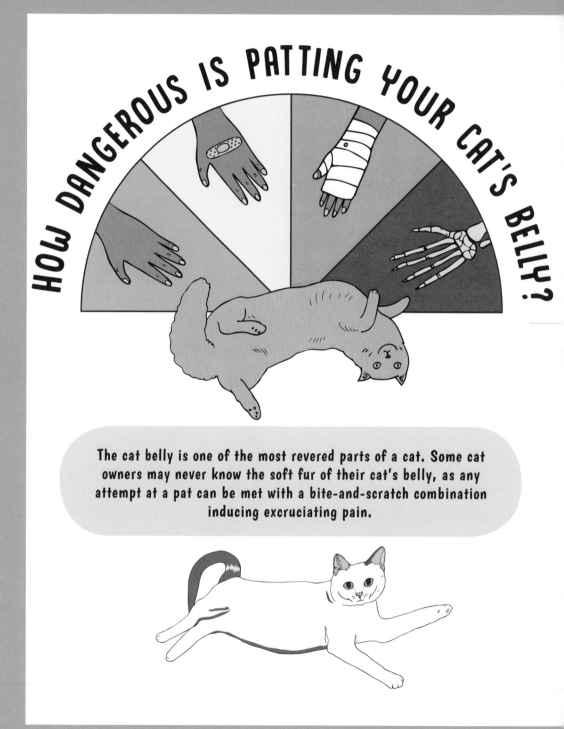

The cat belly is one of the most revered parts of a cat. Some cat owners may never know the soft fur of their cat's belly, as any attempt at a pat can be met with a bite-and-scratch combination inducing excruciating pain.

DO YOU KNOW WHAT THE M MEANS ON A CAT'S FOREHEAD?

It stands for **MYSTERIOUS.**

Even white cats have the M — their fur grows at an angle that makes it visible.

It stands for **METALHEAD.**

It stands for **MONSTER.**

It stands for **MIGHTY.**

It stands for **MAVERICK.**

CAT MODE #1: UNSATISFIED MODE

Unsatisfied mode is when nothing will please me, but I keep wanting things from you. I love to go into this mode at three in the morning.

Now is the time you will discover if your cat can open doors.

I have to tell you about compound interest. It is important and you need to understand it right now.

Shutting the door results in a noise experience that combines yowls and claws with some thumps and bumps in a symphony entitled 'I'm not sleeping so neither are you'. We tried using large couch cushions as a barricade against the door to stop our cat scratching. It did not work.

You assume this late-night wake up is due to hunger, but after stumbling through the house you discover there is plenty of food in kitty's bowl. Your cat wants you to sit with them and pat them while they eat their food for at least ten minutes. You consider setting up a mattress by the cat food.

Glass of water by the bed? ROOKIE MISTAKE. That's the first thing to get knocked off with a quick flick of the paw. But don't assume a water bottle is a foolproof water-drinking method either — kitty will chew the spout, rendering it useless.

AVAILABLE BODY PART BITING OPTIONS:

* feet (summer option only)
* nose
* hair
* wrist
* fingers

CAT MODE #2: SKIDADDLE MODE

You may wonder if I've been drinking red cordial, or maybe I'm trying out a new HIIT workout? Grab a toy and come play with me — I'm ready for fun!

Cats in skidaddle mode often use their claws to pull themselves across the ground along the length of your couch.

Upside-down head and huge pupils are a good indicator your cat has entered skidaddle mode.

Double skidaddle mode can cause mayhem as cats roll into a ball and become one fast-paced kitty unit.

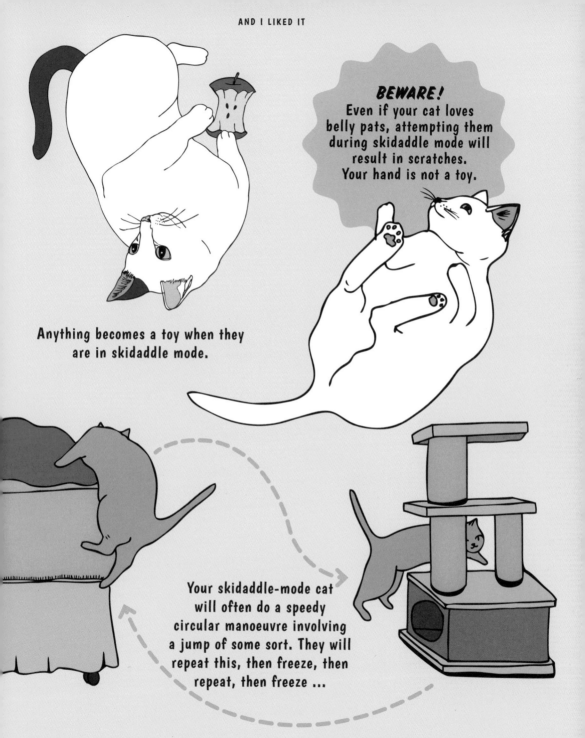

BEWARE!
Even if your cat loves belly pats, attempting them during skidaddle mode will result in scratches. Your hand is not a toy.

Anything becomes a toy when they are in skidaddle mode.

Your skidaddle-mode cat will often do a speedy circular manoeuvre involving a jump of some sort. They will repeat this, then freeze, then repeat, then freeze ...

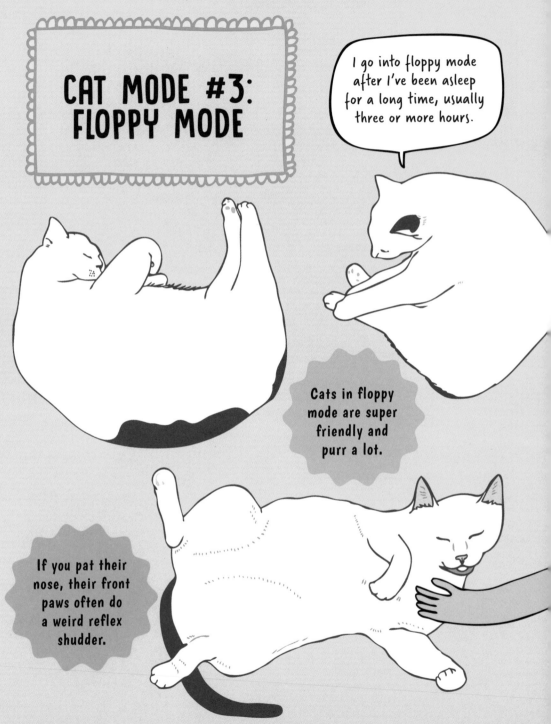

CAT MODE #3: FLOPPY MODE

I go into floppy mode after I've been asleep for a long time, usually three or more hours.

Cats in floppy mode are super friendly and purr a lot.

If you pat their nose, their front paws often do a weird reflex shudder.

They can't stay awake when you're patting them, even if you're making lots of noise.

You can pat their belly and they will not mind.

Their bodies are limp — you can lift up their paws and they just plop down again.

Some cats go on high alert as soon as you go near them. These cats never get into floppy mode.

CAT MODE #4: AGGRESSIVELY AFFECTIONATE MODE

How is this both calming and excruciating at the same time?

I love to show you affection, but sometimes I also like to mix this with some pain.

When cats dig their claws into your legs in a rhythmic way, it is called 'making biscuits'.

You might be patting your cat in their safe zone and they will suddenly decide you have patted them enough and let you know by scratching and biting you.

When they are in aggressively affectionate mode you will hear their loudest purrs.

When you arrive home they will often rub up against your legs in a forceful way, looking for lots of pats.

Some cats might lick and bite your hair. This is a sign of affection but also slightly menacing. Or perhaps they just don't approve of your fruity shampoo?

This is a deep-conditioning massage. Your hair is filthy. You need to lick it clean more often. None of that smelly gunk — use your tongue!

WHAT IS YOUR CAT REALLY SAYING

WHEN THEY GIVE YOU THAT LOOK OF DISDAIN?

end of tail swishes up and down, showing irritation

semi-closed eyes give off an air of aloof superiority

ears pulled back a bit, adding to the sense of unease

when you look at them they look away, demonstrating their judgement

Don't wash things on a warm wash if they're stained. Soak them first, otherwise the warm water sets the stain and it's there forever as a stark reminder of your inability to do the laundry correctly.

ALTERNATE NAMES FOR CAT BREEDS

WOOLLY CURLY LONG BOB

HAIRLESS GOBLIN

ROTUND BLIGHTY PUFF

HIRSUTE FELINE CREATURE

PRINCESS FLUFF-BAE

BASIC ECONOMY FUR CAT

BASIC EXTRA FUR CAT

RUDDERLESS PUDDING PAL

HEFTY CAT BEAST

FLAT-EAR BUBBLE PLOP

MINI EXOTIC JUNGLE CAT

THE ULTIMATE GUIDE TO CAT ACTIVITIES

(I.E. EATING AND SLEEPING)

WHAT DOES YOUR CAT DO ALL DAY?

I often come to my food bowl and wonder why it is empty.

I spend over fifteen hours sleeping.

I spend some time searching for you just after you leave the house. Where have you gone? When will you be coming back?

I walk past the expensive cat bed you got me six months ago, looking for a place to sleep.

Part of my day is spent in beating my personal best for galloping up the length of the house.

SLEEPING WITH A SNUGGLED-UP CAT IS THE BEST WAY TO SLEEP.

There is something magical about having a cat snuggling up near you and feeling cosy and safe.

In winter a cat is like a purring hot water bottle.

The close proximity may result in shared dreams of eating and sleeping.

In the final weeks of my pregnancy, when I was enormous, uncomfortable and overdue, I would wake to Bubsy sleeping across me, keeping me and my unborn child company.

FUNNY THINGS YOUR CAT DOES

drifting when they take a corner really fast

sitting in a box that is too small

falling asleep flat on their back

twisting up into a complicated mess

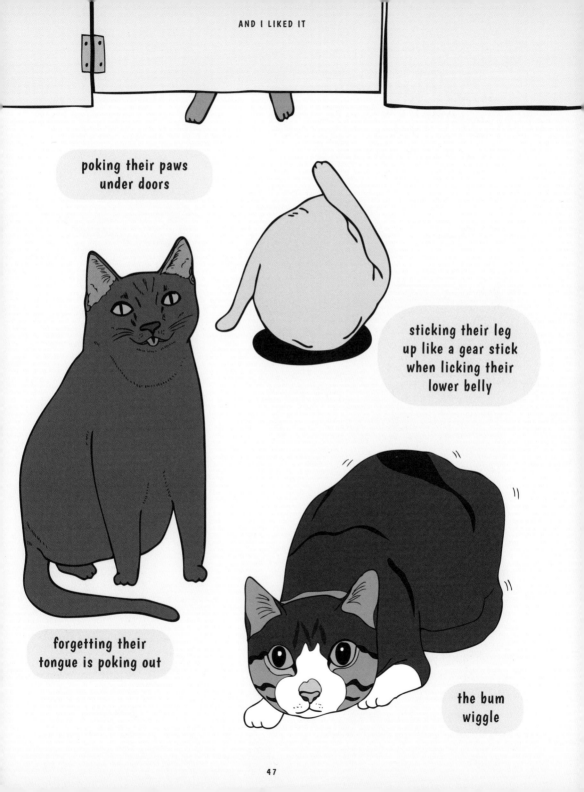

poking their paws under doors

sticking their leg up like a gear stick when licking their lower belly

forgetting their tongue is poking out

the bum wiggle

SUPER CUTE THINGS YOUR CAT DOES

sitting up at the table like a person

hiding all their paws under their body

snuggling in super tight and hugging their heads

standing up on their hind legs

sporting tiny
neckerchiefs

tucking up
their little paws

washing their faces

upside-down head

CATS HAVE MANY SKILLS ...

KITTYTUBE

KITTY SLEEPS FOR 8 HOURS

... but perhaps their most admired is their ability to find a precarious place to sleep while still looking utterly comfortable.

A BRIEF LOOK AT CAT FOOD OVER THE LAST 200 YEARS

And now it's time for a little history lesson. You might even learn something!

Dr Gordon, this food is rather atrocious.

GORDON STABLES

In 1876, a Scottish physician called Gordon Stables wrote a book about cats. Dr Stables recommends oatmeal porridge for kitty's breakfast — for oatmeal is the food of the hero and the poet. Bread soaked in milk is another meal he deems perfect for your puss. For dinner, Dr Stables suggests a wee bit of meat, such as boiled lung. He also writes about how he has seen cats drunk on whisky, so his advice on cat care may be somewhat misguided and out of date.

THE DOMESTIC CAT by Gordon Stables

In the nineteenth and early twentieth centuries, cat food was sold from barrows by people known as 'Cat's Meat Men'.

HORSE MEAT

BASIC WET FOOD

BASIC DRY FOOD

The first commercially available pet food was made by Spratt in the late nineteenth century. In the 1950s the extrusion method was developed to create the dry biscuits still common today.

In the early 1980s gourmet cat food started appearing in tiny tins. The adverts always featured a floofy cat who was a massive food snob.

Ostentatious Cuisine for Puss

CLEAN EATING KITTY

* Instagram worthy
* 35% protein
* random antioxidants
* essential and non-essential fatty acids

All the cool cats eat it!

Specialist cat food is now commonplace, with formulas available for different varieties of cat. Indoor cats, fat cats, cats with furballs, grain-free Paleo cats — you name it, there is a specific feline food available.

YOU KNOW YOUR CAT LOVES TO SLEEP WHEN YOU ARRIVE HOME FROM WORK AND THEY'RE IN THE SAME POSITION AS WHEN YOU LEFT.

8:30 AM – 10:30 AM

Starting with a head cuddle,

10:31 AM – 11:15 AM

**then moving into the classic
paw-pillow pose,**

11:16 AM – 12:10 PM

into another paw-pillow pose,

12:11 AM – 12:31 PM

**followed by a spreading-out sleep
stretch with a crossed paw,**

12:32 PM – 1:36 PM

**now the inward curl with
continued paw cross,**

1:37 PM – 2:59 PM

a 180-degree rotation,

3:00 PM – 4:25 PM

the exposed-belly half turn,

4:26 PM – 5:01 PM

**and completing the day with
a return to head cuddle.**

A CAT'S FAVOURITE PLACES TO SLEEP

on your keyboard when you want to work

in your laundry basket, with a strong preference for just-washed clothes

in a box, because it makes them feel safe and secure

as high up as they can possibly get

in your drawers, with a strong preference for just-washed clothes

TREAT FOOD FOR CATS

pavlova with chunky salmon topping

sticky tuna pudding with salted chicken gravy

giblet cronut

turkey macaron with aspic jelly

Meaty Selections freakshake

Classic Paté in Gravy sliders

Seafood Selections kebab

Tender
Favourites—
topped thin
crust

gravy
ice cream
in a Mixed
Grill cone

beef, liver
and vegetable
cupcake

Korean-
fried
kibble

POTATO CHIPS
WITH TENDER
CHICKEN

MILK
CHOCOLATE
WITH A
GRAVY
CENTRE

LIVER
JUBES

Poultry Platter
loaded fries

chicken-flavour
waffles with
real meaty
chunks

GAMES TO PLAY WITH YOUR CAT

Hide and Seek is an easy one: find a place to hide and pop your head out and then back again quickly. Your cat will want to catch you and possibly eat you.

Tug of War is an old-fashioned romp, often played when you're trying to make your bed and your cat wants to help.

Holes in Boxes is one of the best games for a cat because it involves their most favourite thing: boxes.

WARNING:
Don't stick your fingers in the hole!

AND I LIKED IT

Attach a ribbon to a stick and choreograph a gold medal—worthy rhythmic gymnastics routine with your cat.

KITTY WORLD CUP

Dining Table World Cup is a good way to test if your kitty can bend it like Beckham. A makeshift ball can be created with scrunched-up newspaper.

THE ULTIMATE GUIDE TO CAT LOVERS

HOW DO YOU LET THE WORLD KNOW
YOU'RE A CAT LOVER?

PAWHOUSE
PURRHOUSE

KITTIES
EMPURRIUM

If it's got a
cat on it, I'm
buying it.

BY DECKING YOURSELF OUT IN AS MUCH CAT
PARAPHERNALIA AS YOU CAN.

THE VERY IMPORTANT JOB OF NAMING YOUR CAT

SEA-80

CATRICE STARLING

DICKIE

THE PURRMINATOR
&
SARAH CLAWNER

HER ROYAL HIGHNESS
LA-DI-DA
FINGER BUN SUZETTE

THE ABOMINABLE
SNOW PUSS

CLAWSSANT

PHOELINE

PAWPURRONI

CAT LOVER #1: THE QUINTESSENTIAL CAT LOVER

CAT LOVER #2: THE EXTREME CAT LOVER

In winter the extreme cat lover keeps warm with a layer of bedding made entirely of cats.

When the extreme cat lover is asked how many cats they have and they pause and look embarrassed, it is because they have a lot of cats. You think four is a lot of cats? You are wrong. Thirty-four is a lot of cats.

I've set up a webcam so I can view a live stream of the cats 24/7.

Yes, I know all their names: Muffins, Stuffins, Fluffins, Fruffins, Luffins, Chuffins, Guffins, Puffins, Bluffins, Thuffins, Buffins, Nuffins, Snuffins, Juffins, Ruffins, Xuffins, Bruffins, Quaffins, Druffins, Pruffins, Vruffins, Zuffins, Yuffins, Pluffins, Cruffins, Vuffins, Smuffins, Truffins, Sluffins, Cluffins, Schuffins, Gruffins, Huffins and Wayne.

At work I spend a lot of time looking at cat rescue websites. I want them all!

71

CAT LOVER #3:
THE DIGITAL CAT LOVER

Did you know there are more than two million cat videos on YouTube? The digital cat lover has seen them all.

In 2013 I attended the Internet Cat Video Festival in Minneapolis. It had a cat sculpture made from butter and Keyboard Cat won a lifetime achievement award.

CANNOT CONNECT TO INTERNET

MONTHLY DATA LIMIT REACHED WATCHING A COPIOUS AMOUNT OF CAT VIDEOS

Keyboard Cat is my all-time favourite. I also love Maru and Grumpy Cat and Lil Bub and Snoopy and Hamilton the Hipster Cat and Sam Has Eyebrows.

CAT LOVER #4: THE CAT LOVER TRAPPED INSIDE A DOG LOVER'S BODY

We need to walk him twice a day. It really bugs me when the weather is bad. I wish he just wanted to chill out and sleep all the time.
He barks and yaps all day long. I wish he made a different noise, something soothing, like a soft rhythmic buzz.
My little plastic bag is full of poop. Surely there must be a better option, like a tray of poop I can keep in my laundry?
Every day the cat lover trapped inside a dog lover's body washes their dog, and every day they wish their dog could just lick themselves clean.

WHEN A CAT PARENT BECOMES A HUMAN PARENT

Having kids is a great way to trial if you're up for the job of looking after a cat.

You may actually catch your cat eye-rolling your baby. Your cat views your baby as a pathetic, lap-hogging creature who cannot even walk. The baby is surely not worthy of all that lap time.

In a few short months, your kid and your cat will both think that the other's name is 'Gentle Hands'.

Need some thrills? Combine a baby who loves to climb with a sky-high scratching post. The day you realise they have learnt to climb it will be the day you have kittens.

Try keeping your cat out of these contraptions. Impossible. They basically belong to your cat now.

Why not take your pram for a test run? Your cat will look like royalty, perched up in their Roman chariot.

WHY GO OUT WHEN YOU CAN STAY IN WITH YOUR CAT?

Forget FOMO — you need JOKO in your life: the joy of kitting out.

Enjoy a relaxing bath while you both listen to some podcasts.

Baking treats is always good fun, especially when you have a kitty cook helping with some furry additions to make the flavour really pop.

THE ULTIMATE GUIDE TO CAT SPOTTING

the cat up a tree

the cat in a shop

the cat that runs off but then comes back for a pat

the scaredy-cat

the cat that lets you pat its belly

the gang of kittens

ULTIMATE CAT SPOT #1: THE GRAND CANYON, USA

My ultimate cat spot occurred in 2013 while travelling across the USA. We arrived at the Grand Canyon and heard meowing. We then spotted a couple with their cat in what looked like a custom-built backpack.

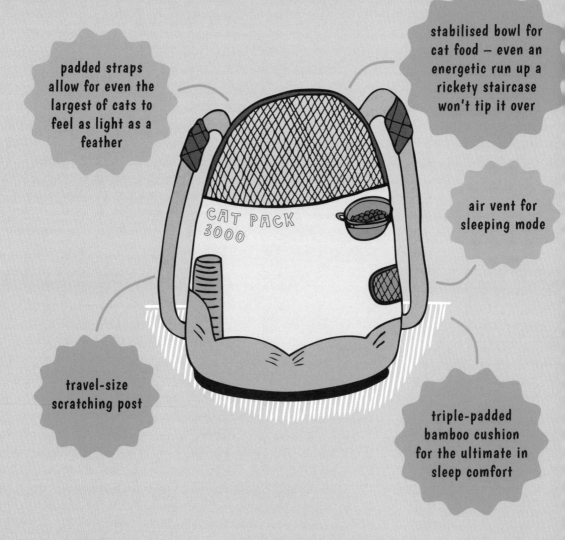

stabilised bowl for cat food — even an energetic run up a rickety staircase won't tip it over

padded straps allow for even the largest of cats to feel as light as a feather

air vent for sleeping mode

travel-size scratching post

triple-padded bamboo cushion for the ultimate in sleep comfort

CAT PACK 3000

ULTIMATE CAT SPOT #2:
LARGO DI TORRE ARGENTINA, ITALY

You can pick up a souvenir at the gift shop. We got this mug.

In 2010 we were walking around Rome, eating food, thinking the pizza would be the best part of the day, when I spotted a cat on a fence. Suddenly we started seeing more and more, and when we looked down into the ancient ruins where Julius Caesar was killed, we discovered that it was full of kitties. The ruins are now home to a cat sanctuary for sick and homeless cats.

GATTI ROMA
TORRE ARGENTINA CAT SANC

ALL THE BEST HOLIDAY ACCOMMODATION INVOLVES CATS.

MEMPHIS

LONDON

LIMA

Kyoto

CAPE TOWN

BIRMINGHAM, UK

A FEW OF THE CATS I'VE MET ON MY TRAVELS:

SYDNEY, AUSTRALIA

MEMPHIS, USA

LONDON, UK

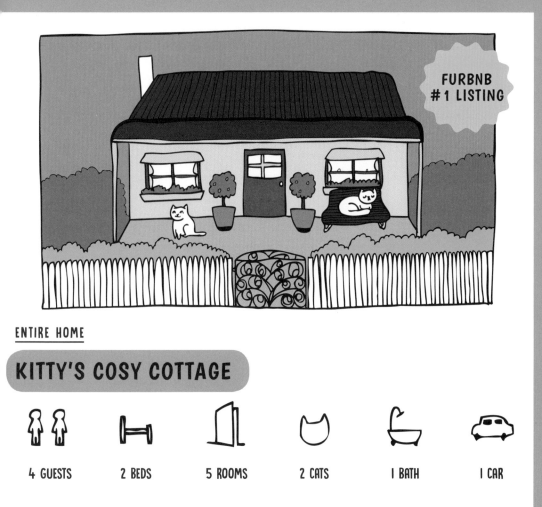

ENTIRE HOME

KITTY'S COSY COTTAGE

4 GUESTS	2 BEDS	5 ROOMS	2 CATS	1 BATH	1 CAR

Cute two-bedroom cottage surrounded by lush garden and occupied by two lovely white cats.

The cats will welcome you into the cottage and show you where the key safe is located. They will meow to you the correct combination to unlock the cottage.

The cats will keep you warm by sitting on your lap in front of the open fireplace, provide a full English breakfast each morning, and offer a turn-down service for an extra ten pats per day.

SPOT HUNDREDS OF CATS AT YOUR LOCAL CAT SHOW

OH MY FREAKING GOSH. There are wall-to-wall cats here.

WHAT DO JUDGES LOOK FOR?

ears are pointed and large

neck is medium length

head should be longer than it is wide

tail fur is long and tapered

paws are large and round

legs are long and straight

UTH

What does the 'UTH' sign mean on this cat's enclosure?

Oh, 'Unable To be Handled'. This cat probably bit a judge. Jings!

WHERE WERE YOU THE FIRST TIME YOU SPOTTED A NORWEGIAN FOREST CAT?

At a cat cafe in Nottingham? Researching tigers for a school project and staring, mouth agape, at the image search results for 'big cat'? Dropping your cat off to a cat boarding facility and finding one in the next enclosure? You always remember the first time you spot this amazing breed.

large almond eyes

thick tufts of fur in ears

long, thick double coat that changes with the seasons

big, fluffy tail

tufts of fur between the toes of their giant paws

Norwegian Forest cats can weigh up to 10 kilograms, but 6 kilograms of that is probably fur.

VISITING FRIENDS WITH CATS

THE HAPPY FEELINGS YOU GET WHEN YOU SPOT A CAT ON THE TV

THE ULTIMATE GUIDE TO MAGICAL CAT DISCOVERIES

KITTY HEAD BUMPS

When we arrive home we get down on the floor to give our cat head bumps.

Head-bumping sessions can last a few minutes, with multiple bumps occurring in this time. They are usually accompanied with friendly 'broowww' meows and purring.

Certain front-on head bumps can be turned into a nose-on-nose pat, where you move your nose up and down to pat your cat's nose.

Our kids have picked up this habit, and for a while our eldest kid thought a head bump was an acceptable greeting for all animals.

Sometimes the bump is a swift in and out, other times it is a solid joining of the foreheads for a moment.

THE CAT SNUGGLE

When multiple cats are involved in a snuggle it is called a 'Kitty Club Cuddle'.

On rare occasions the cat snuggle can represent ancient Taoist symbols.

It is commonplace to not know whose paws are whose during a snuggle.

Sometimes cats incorporate objects into the snuggle.

Often one cat will use another cat as a pillow.

UNIQUE PRODUCTS YOU CAN BUY YOUR CAT

Not interested in looking at your cat's poo area? Decorate it with a fancy jewel.

INFLATABLE CAT UNICORN HORN

Wanting to live the jetsetter lifestyle but your cat is holding you back? Transport them in some fancy luggage.

A great way to make your cat loathe every fibre of your being.

How much screen time is too much for your cat? Who knows, but watching them beat their top score on an iPad game is super cute.

Neutered your cat but miss their busty ball sack? Neuticles are testicular implants for cats, so they still look intact.

Does your cat think they are a dog? You can now walk them around the neighbourhood.

TOILET TRAINING FOR CATS

Do you want your cat sitting on the toilet to poop? Teach them with this kit.

A TV-shaped bird feeder always plays your cat's favourite channel.

Cat scratching posts are too simple — your cat needs a fully kittened-out treehouse.

CAT AND DOG BEST FRIENDS

Cats and dogs are usually thought of as mortal enemies. However, people who spend a lot of time on the internet know this isn't always the case. Cats and dogs can be best friends and it is the cutest thing ever.

CAT AND DOG BEST FRIENDS

WATCH NOW
FLUFFY FRIENDS FOREVER

UP NEXT

YouTube is full of hundreds of videos of cats and dogs that love each other.

They protect each other.

ONE DAY YOU WILL DISCOVER THAT YOUR REGULAR-SIZED KITTY LOOKS POSITIVELY GINORMOUS FROM ONE PARTICULAR ANGLE.

DISCOVER THE HIDDEN BENEFIT OF A CAT ON YOUR LAP

And in feline-related news, an orange cat has caused havoc today on the set of Kathy and Randy's popular morning show.

Everyone around you is required to fetch you things!

DR CAT IS IN THE HOUSE, READY TO LOOK AFTER YOUR HEALTH AND WELLBEING.

Studies have shown that the frequency of a cat's purr, between 20 and 140 Hz, can help stimulate healing in bones and muscles, lower the risk of heart attacks and decrease the symptoms of dyspnoea.

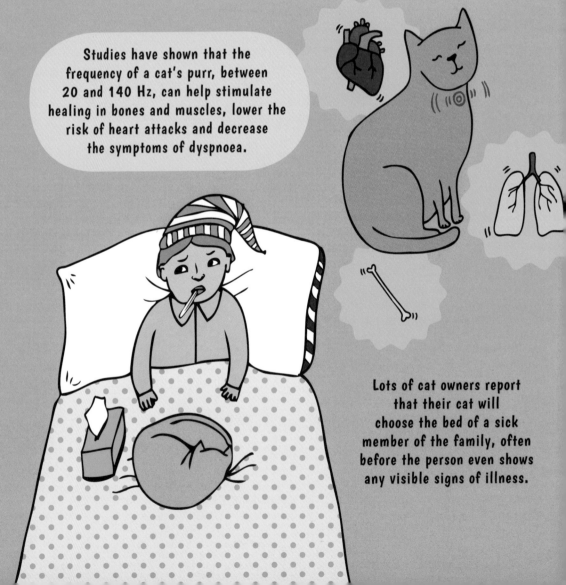

Lots of cat owners report that their cat will choose the bed of a sick member of the family, often before the person even shows any visible signs of illness.

Ginger normally gives Felicity's lap a 5-metre berth, but Felicity's hCG levels are at 18 mIU/mL and suddenly Ginger thinks Felicity's lap is the best place ever.

A home pregnancy test won't give Felicity a positive reading until the hCG levels reach at least 20 mIU/mL.

Until then, Felicity will assume she has a funny tummy and Ginger has finally turned into the lap cat she always wanted.

Cats are like a home pregnancy test — just don't pee on them, please.

SALTY CRISPS

SICK

WELCOME TO THE WONDERFUL WORLD OF THE CAT CAFE

Originating in Taiwan and becoming famous in Japan, the cat cafe concept is now popping up all over the world. Its success is obvious when you consider that they have the perfect business model: combining food and felines.

KITTEA CAFE
CUSTOMER LOYALTY CARD

CAT CAFE RULES:

* No flash photography.
* No climbing on the cat equipment.
* Don't wake the cats, otherwise they will get grumpy.
* Don't pick up the cats.
* If a cat is sitting in a chair and you want to sit there, wait for them to move.

You don't go to a cat cafe for the snacks. Due to health and safety it's often just pre-packaged biscuits and a few drink options.

HOW TO THROW A PARTY FOR YOUR CAT

Woohoo, I love to party!

REASONS TO THROW A KITTY PARTY:

* It's their birthday!
* They're cute and you need to celebrate!
* It's Tuesday!

CHOOSE A FUN PARTY THEME:

I'm here for the Ugly Kitty Sweater Party!

The Great Kittish Bake Off Party

Welcome to the Catsino Royale Party. Ready to play some purrker?

Creating a cake for your cat is easy — just open a couple of cans of cat food and stick them on top of each other. Add some dry cat food for a fancy finish.

The perfect gift for a cat is a large empty box with fancy gift wrapping and multiple holes.

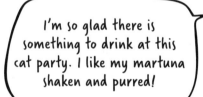

I'm so glad there is something to drink at this cat party. I like my martuna shaken and purred!

CHATPAGNE

meowshake

WHISKERY

THE FUTURE OF CATS

Fearing a loss in market share for videos on YouTube, cats start aspirational lifestyle vlogs offering tips on speed cleaning your house, make-up contouring, shopping hauls and morning, evening and night routines.

Watch out, birds!

MY MORNING ROUTINE
👍 234 👎 15
SUBSCRIBE

Heat-emitting paw pads help cats levitate off the ground. Tail moves left and right to steer.

ACKNOWLEDGEMENTS

I would like to thank Emily Hart for her support in editing this book and Pam Brewster for her editorial supervision. Thanks also go to designers Andy Warren and Jessica Lowe for their talent and enthusiasm.

Thank you to my partner, Gareth, who held up the fort while I spent months drawing cats.

To my two kids, Clyde and Dougie, for showing solid enthusiasm for cats from the get-go.

Thank you to Annabel, Eliza, Vijay and Gareth for reading my drafts and offering valuable feedback.

And thanks to all the other cat lovers out there who share my passion for cats.